Knowledge of SELF (Social Empowerment Learning Framework)

Young Adult Edition (Ages 18–21)

Facilitator's Guide

Written by Cedric A. Washington

Table of Contents

- # Unit One: SELF Conscience

  - Lesson 1: Am I a Color? (Part 1)
  - Lesson 2: Am I a Color? (Part 2)
  - Lesson 3: Love Yourself — The Skin You're In
  - Lesson 4: Attributes/Characteristics of SELF
  - Lesson 5: Ethics
  - Lesson 6: Image
  - Lesson 7: Achievements

- # Unit Two: SELF Governing

  - Lesson 1: Health and Nutrition
  - Lesson 2: The Importance of FOCUS
  - Lesson 3: Role Modeling
  - Lesson 4: Hygiene
  - Lesson 5: Emotional Maturity
  - Lesson 6: Puberty and Self-Respect
  - Lesson 7: Peer Pressure

- # Unit Three: Social Conscience

  - Lesson 1: How to Be Effective in Your Community
  - Lesson 2: African American Leaders
  - Lesson 3: Hip Hop: The Culture
  - Lesson 4: Family Dynamics
  - Lesson 5: Accountability
  - Lesson 6: Community Service and Giving Back
  - Lesson 7: Building Your Legacy

- # Unit Four: Aspirations

  - Lesson 1: What I Want to Be When I Grow Up
  - Lesson 2: Career Day Panel Preparation and Event
  - Lesson 3: Resume Workshop
  - Lesson 4: Short Term Goals
  - Lesson 5: Long Term Goals
  - Lesson 6: Financial Literacy
  - Lesson 7: Building Wealth and Generational Legacy

- # Unit Five: Good People Skills

  - Lesson 1: Conflict Resolution
  - Lesson 2: Group Cooperation

Table of Contents... Continued.

TM

Knowledge
of S.E.L.F.
Curriculum

Knowledge of SELF Curriculum — Young Adult Facilitator's Guide

© 2025 by Cedric A. Washington

Who Lives Like This?! Publishing LLC
www.nerdyouthservices.org

ISBN: 978-1-970680-14-0 (Paperback)

Cover design and interior layout by
Who Lives Like This?! Publishing LLC Design Team

Printed in the United States of America

First Edition — 2025

About the Author

Cedric A. Washington is a master educator, speaker, author, former college basketball player, and the Executive Director of NERD Youth Services, Inc. A native of Gary, Indiana. Over two decades of experience in education, mentoring, and community leadership have fueled his commitment to building culturally responsive, empowering programs for African American youth. As the visionary behind the Knowledge of SELF (Social Empowerment Learning Framework) curriculum, Cedric blends historical awareness, emotional intelligence, leadership training, and personal reflection to cultivate greatness in every student he reaches. His work has been celebrated nationally at education conferences, faith institutions, and youth leadership summits. Cedric's mission is simple but powerful: To equip young people with the self-knowledge, discipline, and purpose they need to transform themselves — and the world.

Knowledge of SELF Curriculum

Bonus Tools & Supporting Resources

Middle School, High School, and Young Adult Editions

By Cedric A. Washington

"Speak it. Believe it. Do it."

Daily Affirmations

I AM a trailblazer. I AM destined to succeed. Speak it. Believe it. Do it. – Cedric A. Washington

- I am enough, just as I am.
- My history is powerful, my future is greater.
- I am not what the world calls me—I am who God created me to be.
- I will lead with love, courage, and clarity.
- My skin, my hair, my mind—divinely designed.
- I rise above every label and lie.
- Greatness is not ahead of me; it's within me.
- I walk in wisdom and purpose.
- I am part of a legacy of excellence.
- I build, I uplift, I transform.

Icebreaker Activity Bank

Identity Shields

Students draw a shield divided into 4 parts: family, culture, goals, and values.

Affirmation Circle

Each student shares one positive word about themselves. Then peers affirm each person.

If You Really Knew Me

In a safe circle, students complete the sentence: 'If you really knew me, you'd know...'

Who's in Your Circle?

Draw a circle of influence. Identify family, friends, mentors who shape your SELF.

Two Truths and a Dream

Students share two true things about themselves and one aspirational goal.

Pre-Reflection Survey

Before starting the Knowledge of SELF curriculum, please answer honestly:

1. What do you currently know about your cultural identity?

2. How confident are you in making positive decisions for your future? (1–5)

3. What does success mean to you?

4. Have you ever felt misunderstood in school or in life? Explain.

5. What do you hope to gain from this experience?

Post-Reflection Survey

After completing the Knowledge of SELF curriculum, reflect on the following:

1. What is something new you learned about yourself?

2. How has your definition of success changed?

3. What parts of your identity do you embrace more now than before?

4. What are three personal goals you now feel ready to achieve?

5. How will you use what you've learned to uplift others?

Certificate of Completion

This certifies that

_____

has successfully completed the

Knowledge of SELF Curriculum

Middle School / High School / Young Adult Edition

Led by: _____

Date: _____

Created by Cedric A. Washington | "Speak it. Believe it. Do it."

Knowledge of SELF (Social Empowerment Learning Framework)

Young Adult Edition (Ages 18–25) — Facilitator's Guide

Unit One: SELF Conscience

Lesson 1: Am I a Color? (Part 1)

Objective:
Guide students in critically examining the historical evolution of racial identity labels and their impact on self-perception.

Do Now:
Ask students: "Do you identify yourself as African American? What does that mean to you?"

Facilitator Talk:
- Introduce the history of terms: Negro, Colored, Black, African American, Afro American.
- Differentiate between Ethnicity and Nationality.
- Discuss how miseducation around identity affects self-worth.

Key Discussion Questions:
1. How do labels shape how we see ourselves and how others see us?
2. Can a person truly know themselves if they don't understand the history behind their identity?

Activity:
- Lead students through an exploration of identity labels.
- Have them write a reflection about reclaiming their identity.

Real World Connection:
Connect students' identity exploration to broader conversations about cultural pride and leadership.

Reflection Journal:
Prompt students to write two full paragraphs on what reclaiming their true identity means to them.

Lesson 2: Am I a Color? (Part 2)

Objective:
Deepen students' understanding of historical identity through biblical references and cultural reflection.

Do Now:
Ask students: "What is the purpose of school? What is the purpose of church?"

Facilitator Talk:
- Emphasize that pre-slavery history is in the Bible: Genesis, Exodus, Deuteronomy, Revelation.
- Discuss why history often starts at slavery in textbooks and the importance of challenging that.

Key Discussion Questions:
1. Why is it important to question where history "starts" in school textbooks?
2. How does biblical history strengthen or challenge what you thought about your identity?

Activity:
- Scriptural study (Deuteronomy 28) on prophecy and historical context.

Real World Connection:
Encourage students to see themselves in the context of a much longer, richer history.

Reflection Journal:
Prompt students to reflect in two full paragraphs about their emotions and new perspectives on identity.

Lesson 3: Love Yourself — The Skin You're In

Objective:
Help students embrace their unique skin tones, understand the scientific power of melanin, and dismantle negative self-perceptions.

Do Now:
Ask students: "How do you feel about your skin tone today?"

Facilitator Talk:
- Teach that melanin is the biological foundation of dominance and survival, not inferiority.
- Discuss the true scientific meaning of 666 (6 protons, 6 neutrons, 6 electrons).
- Introduce the Skin Tone Chart activity.

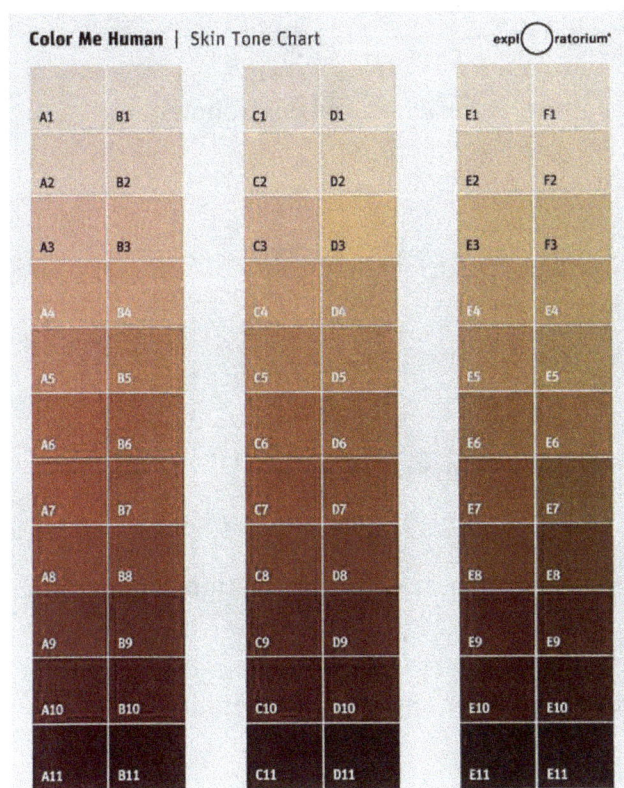

Color Me Human | Skin Tone Chart   expl◯ratorium®

A1	B1		C1	D1		E1	F1
A2	B2		C2	D2		E2	F2
A3	B3		C3	D3		E3	F3
A4	B4		C4	D4		E4	E4
A5	B5		C5	D5		E5	E5
A6	B6		C6	D6		E6	E6
A7	B7		C7	D7		E7	E7
A8	B8		C8	D8		E8	E8
A9	B9		C9	D9		E9	E9
A10	B10		C10	D10		E10	E10
A11	B11		C11	D11		E11	E11

Key Discussion Questions:
1. Why are we taught color labels that distort our natural beauty?
2. How can understanding your biology change your self-esteem?

Activity:
- Have students match their skin tone on the Skin Tone Chart.
- Facilitate a discussion about the real power of melanin.

Real World Connection:
Help students understand how redefining self-image impacts future success and resilience.

Reflection Journal:
Prompt students to reflect in two full paragraphs on the power of loving their authentic selves.

Lesson 4: Attributes/Characteristics of SELF

Objective:
Help students identify their innate attributes and build their self-definition based on truth, not stereotypes.

Do Now:
Ask students: "List three traits that you admire most about yourself."

Facilitator Talk:
- Discuss how characteristics are shaped by culture, experience, and environment.
- Challenge students to think beyond labels assigned by others.

Key Discussion Questions:
1. Why is it important to define yourself rather than let society define you?
2. How do your attributes connect to your purpose?

Activity:
- Self-Inventory: List 5 strengths and 2 areas of growth.
- Discuss how knowing your strengths shapes decision-making.

Real World Connection:
Connect personal attributes to career choices, leadership, and healthy relationships.

Reflection Journal:
Prompt students to reflect in two full paragraphs on their top three self-defining traits.

Lesson 5: Ethics

Objective:
Students will explore personal values and how ethics guide behavior, leadership, and legacy.

Do Now:
Ask students: "What are three non-negotiable values you live by?"

Facilitator Talk:
- Define ethics as the moral compass that governs actions.
- Explain how values determine the strength of one's leadership and legacy.

Key Discussion Questions:
1. How do ethics protect your integrity?
2. Why is it important to stay committed to your values, even under pressure?

Activity:
- Value Sorting: Students rank 10 values in order of importance.
- Small group discussion on why different people value different things.

Real World Connection:
Discuss ethical leadership and how it's needed across industries and communities.

Reflection Journal:
Prompt students to reflect in two full paragraphs about a time when their ethics were tested.

Lesson 6: Image

Objective:
Students will analyze how personal image impacts perception and opportunity while emphasizing authenticity.

Do Now:
Ask students: "Do you believe your image impacts your opportunities? Why or why not?"

Facilitator Talk:
- Discuss the difference between "authentic image" vs. "manufactured image."
- Image is not about pretending — it's about presenting your truth with pride.

Key Discussion Questions:
1. How does the way you carry yourself reflect your inner SELF?
2. Why must authenticity be part of your image?

Activity:
- Image Reflection Exercise: Compare personal/public personas.
- Group sharing (optional).

Real World Connection:
Relate image to professional branding and real-world leadership opportunities.

Reflection Journal:
Prompt students to write two full paragraphs about how they want to shape their authentic image.

Lesson 7: Achievements

Objective:
Students will reflect on past achievements and set intentions for future accomplishments.

Do Now:
Ask students: "What achievement are you most proud of so far?"

Facilitator Talk:
- Discuss the importance of celebrating milestones.
- Achievements are not accidents — they are results of focus, faith, and work.

Key Discussion Questions:
1. Why must you celebrate your small wins along the journey?
2. How do your past achievements reveal patterns of your greatness?

Activity:
- Achievement Timeline: Create a timeline marking personal milestones.

Real World Connection:
Tie achievement to resume building, personal branding, and future leadership.

Reflection Journal:
Prompt students to reflect in two full paragraphs on how past wins fuel future goals.

Knowledge of SELF (Social Empowerment Learning Framework)

Young Adult Edition (Ages 18–21) — Facilitator's Guide

Unit Two: SELF Governing

Lesson 1: Health and Nutrition

Objective:
Guide students to understand the necessity of physical wellness, nutrition, and holistic health practices for leadership and life success.

Do Now:
Ask students: "What is one health habit you want to start or strengthen?"

Facilitator Talk:
- Discuss foundational health practices: hydration, sea moss, clean eating, exercise.
- The body is the first tool of mastery — protect and honor it.

Key Discussion Questions:
1. How does physical health support your mental and emotional strength?
2. Why should health be viewed as revolutionary self-love?

Activity:
- Create a weekly health action plan.
- Include one nutrition upgrade, one new physical activity, and one self-care habit.

Real World Connection:
Relate health discipline to leadership effectiveness, longevity, and generational wellness.

Reflection Journal:
Prompt students to reflect in two full paragraphs on how they will honor their health this season.

Lesson 2: The Importance of FOCUS

Objective:
Lead students through the revolutionary F.O.C.U.S. process: Fallback, Opportunities, Cultivate, Understanding, Succeed.

Do Now:
Ask students: "Why is staying focused a major challenge today?"

Facilitator Talk:
- Break down F.O.C.U.S.:
  - Fallback: Withdraw from distractions.
  - Opportunities: Align with positive spaces and people.
  - Cultivate: Work the dream daily.
  - Understanding: Not everyone will "get" your journey.
  - Succeed: Celebrate small wins.

Key Discussion Questions:
1. Why must you sometimes separate to elevate?
2. How does understanding that not everyone will understand empower your grind?

Activity:
- Create a F.O.C.U.S. Vision Map for one major goal.

Real World Connection:
Tie the F.O.C.U.S. method to entrepreneurship, education, athletics, and leadership.

Reflection Journal:
Prompt students to write two full paragraphs: "What will I Fallback from to FOCUS on my future?"

Lesson 3: Role Modeling

Objective:
Instill the mindset that leadership is lived daily through words, actions, and quiet influence.

Do Now:
Ask students: "Who do you believe looks up to you today?"

Facilitator Talk:
- Role modeling happens even when we don't realize it.
- Your life is someone else's survival guide.

Key Discussion Questions:
1. Why is leadership about action, not just titles?
2. How does living your truth empower others silently?

Activity:
- Legacy Role Model List: Students list 5 ways they want to inspire others.

Real World Connection:
Discuss how role modeling opens doors: jobs, scholarships, mentorship, opportunities.

Reflection Journal:
Prompt students to write two full paragraphs about what legacy their daily actions are building.

Lesson 4: Hygiene

Objective:
Teach students that daily hygiene is an act of self-respect, professionalism, and cultural excellence.

Do Now:
Ask students: "How does taking care of your body show love for yourself and respect for others?"

Facilitator Talk:
- Hygiene is leadership made visible.
- Consistent habits reflect discipline, pride, and self-mastery.

Key Discussion Questions:
1. How does personal hygiene impact confidence and opportunities?
2. Why is hygiene more than appearance — but a statement of value?

Activity:
- Hygiene Best Practices Checklist: Create a personal hygiene routine blueprint.

Real World Connection:
Link hygiene discipline to first impressions, professional spaces, and leadership influence.

Reflection Journal:
Prompt students to write two full paragraphs about the connection between self-care and self-respect.

Lesson 5: Emotional Maturity

Objective:
Guide students to develop emotional discipline, resilience, and responsibility.

Do Now:
Ask students: "When was a time you could have handled your emotions better?"

Facilitator Talk:
- Emotional maturity isn't about suppressing feelings — it's about managing them wisely.
- Leaders respond; they don't react.

Key Discussion Questions:
1. Why is emotional maturity a superpower?
2. How does emotional maturity protect your vision and relationships?

Activity:
- Trigger Map: Identify emotional triggers and healthy coping strategies.

Real World Connection:
Discuss how emotional intelligence is a key leadership trait in careers, relationships, and entrepreneurship.

Reflection Journal:
Prompt students to reflect in two full paragraphs on a plan for growing their emotional maturity.

Lesson 6: Puberty and Self-Respect

Objective:
Provide young adults with a strong foundation for embracing bodily changes, self-respect, and identity growth.

Do Now:
Ask students: "What advice would you give your younger self about growing up?"

Facilitator Talk:
- Puberty is a sacred transformation, not a shameful event.
- Self-respect begins with body awareness, emotional honesty, and wise boundaries.

Key Discussion Questions:
1. How can understanding your body protect your health and self-esteem?
2. Why is positive self-talk crucial during transitional stages of growth?

Activity:
- Growth Affirmation Letters: Students write a letter celebrating their growth journey.

Real World Connection:
Connect body positivity and self-awareness to mental health, leadership, and life resilience.

Reflection Journal:
Prompt students to write two full paragraphs reflecting on how growth has shaped their identity.

Lesson 7: Peer Pressure

Objective:
Equip students to recognize peer pressure and build inner strength to stand firm in their purpose.

Do Now:
Ask students: "What makes it hard to say 'no' sometimes, even when you know you should?"

Facilitator Talk:
- Peer pressure can be loud or silent.
- True leadership sometimes means standing alone.

Key Discussion Questions:
1. Why does standing on your principles sometimes cost popularity?
2. How can you support others in resisting negative peer pressure?

Activity:
- Refusal Skill Role-Plays: Practice ways to respectfully decline negative influence.

Real World Connection:
Tie peer resistance to leadership training, entrepreneurship, and future independence.

Reflection Journal:
Prompt students to reflect in two full paragraphs about how they will navigate peer pressure with power.

Knowledge of SELF (Social Empowerment Learning Framework)

Young Adult Edition (Ages 18–21) — Facilitator's Guide

Unit Three: Social Conscience

Lesson 1: How to Be Effective in Your Community

Objective:
Empower students to understand that personal transformation fuels community transformation.

Do Now:
Ask students: "Name one positive change you wish to see in your community."

Facilitator Talk:
- Change doesn't start in systems; it starts in hearts.
- Leadership is not waiting for permission — it's taking action where you stand.

Key Discussion Questions:
1. Why must we build instead of just complain?
2. How does serving your community strengthen your identity?

Activity:
- Community Action Blueprint: Students outline one project they could realistically launch.

Real World Connection:
Connect personal purpose to civic responsibility, entrepreneurship, and social impact.

Reflection Journal:
Prompt students to reflect in two full paragraphs on one change they are committed to creating.

Lesson 2: African American Leaders

Objective:
Inspire students through the lives and legacies of Black leaders who exemplified courage, wisdom, and purpose.

Do Now:
Ask students: "Who is one Black leader who inspires you? Why?"

Facilitator Talk:
- Discuss diverse leaders: Marcus Garvey, Angela Davis, Malcolm X, Fred Hampton, and more.
- Leadership is sacrifice, vision, and legacy.

Key Discussion Questions:
1. What sacrifices did these leaders make for the greater good?
2. How can you lead in your generation differently because of their examples?

Activity:
- Legacy Analysis: Students research a leader and present key takeaways.

Real World Connection:
Tie leadership study to activism, business innovation, politics, and community organization.

Reflection Journal:
Prompt students to reflect in two full paragraphs about the leader they relate to most and why.

Lesson 3: Hip Hop: The Culture

Objective:
Guide students in understanding Hip Hop as a global cultural movement rooted in resistance, storytelling, and empowerment.

Do Now:
Ask students: "What Hip Hop song or artist has taught you something powerful?"

Facilitator Talk:
- Hip Hop is not just entertainment — it's education, activism, and storytelling.
- True Hip Hop challenges oppression, uplifts communities, and inspires movements.

Key Discussion Questions:
1. How did Hip Hop give a voice to the voiceless?
2. Why must we protect the roots of our culture from exploitation?

Activity:
- Cultural Impact Project: Students analyze a Hip Hop piece that carries a powerful message.

Real World Connection:
Connect Hip Hop to entrepreneurship, journalism, activism, and education.

Reflection Journal:
Prompt students to reflect in two full paragraphs about how Hip Hop has shaped their identity and vision.

Lesson 4: Family Dynamics

Objective:
Help students explore how family structures and experiences shape personal identity, community leadership, and generational patterns.

Do Now:
Ask students: "What is one positive trait you inherited from your family?"

Facilitator Talk:
- Families are the first classrooms.
- Healing family wounds creates stronger communities.

Key Discussion Questions:
1. How do family dynamics impact your sense of leadership and belonging?
2. Why must we heal before we build?

Activity:
- Family Reflection Tree: Students map out values they want to continue and those they want to transform.

Real World Connection:
Relate family reflection to future parenting, mentoring, leadership, and breaking generational cycles.

Reflection Journal:
Prompt students to reflect in two full paragraphs about the type of legacy they want their family to create.

Lesson 5: Accountability

Objective:
Guide students to embrace accountability as a necessary pillar for leadership, respect, and personal growth.

Do Now:
Ask students: "What is one area of life you take full ownership of?"

Facilitator Talk:
- Accountability means owning your actions, your growth, and your greatness.
- Excuses delay destiny.

Key Discussion Questions:
1. Why is accountability crucial for building trust and power?
2. How does blaming others rob you of your ability to change?

Activity:
- Accountability Contract: Students identify one area of life where they will step up ownership.

Real World Connection:
Connect accountability to leadership roles, entrepreneurship, activism, and generational wealth.

Reflection Journal:
Prompt students to reflect in two full paragraphs about the power of personal responsibility.

Lesson 6: Community Service and Giving Back

Objective:
Inspire students to see service not as charity but as revolution — a way to sow seeds for lasting change.

Do Now:
Ask students: "What cause or issue would you dedicate your time to solving?"

Facilitator Talk:
- Giving back builds the village.
- Service sharpens leadership, expands influence, and multiplies blessings.

Key Discussion Questions:
1. Why is serving your people revolutionary?
2. How does service sharpen your gifts and leadership?

Activity:
- Create a Service Blueprint: Students design a service project plan based on their passion.

Real World Connection:
Relate service to nonprofit leadership, social entrepreneurship, and civic empowerment.

Reflection Journal:
Prompt students to reflect in two full paragraphs on how they will serve and sow into their communities.

Lesson 7: Building Your Legacy

Objective:
Lead students to intentionally craft their life's impact and purpose, leaving a mark that transcends generations.

Do Now:
Ask students: "What do you want to be remembered for 100 years from now?"

Facilitator Talk:
- Legacy is built in daily decisions.
- You are writing history now — live accordingly.

Key Discussion Questions:
1. Why must legacy be intentional, not accidental?
2. How do your current actions echo into future generations?

Activity:
- Legacy Vision Board: Students create a board mapping their desired personal and community impact.

Real World Connection:
Tie legacy building to entrepreneurship, education, politics, mentorship, and family.

Reflection Journal:
Prompt students to reflect in two full paragraphs about their life's mission and legacy blueprint.

Knowledge of SELF (Social Empowerment Learning Framework)

Young Adult Edition (Ages 18–21) — Facilitator's Guide

Unit Four: Aspirations

Lesson 1: What I Want to Be When I Grow Up

Objective:
Lead students to envision a purpose-driven future aligned with their talents, passions, and cultural responsibility.

Do Now:
Ask students: "If you could create any career or life path, what would it be?"

Facilitator Talk:
- You are not just building a career — you are building a mission.
- Purpose is greater than paychecks.

Key Discussion Questions:
1. Why is it important to align career choices with passion and purpose?
2. How does your dream job serve your people, not just yourself?

Activity:
- Dream Career Map: Students design pathways for their aspirations.

Real World Connection:
Relate career building to community needs, entrepreneurship, and economic independence.

Reflection Journal:
Prompt students to reflect in two full paragraphs about how their dreams can heal and build their community.

Lesson 2: Career Day Panel Preparation and Event

Objective:
Prepare students to engage, network, and learn from professionals in fields aligned with their dreams.

Do Now:
Ask students: "What question would you ask someone already living your dream life?"

Facilitator Talk:
- Exposure expands expectation.
- Networking is relationship-building, not just opportunity-hunting.

Key Discussion Questions:
1. Why is proximity to success powerful?
2. How does learning from others speed up your own journey?

Activity:
- Career Day Prep: Students create questions for panelists and prepare to introduce themselves professionally.

Real World Connection:
Discuss how strategic relationships open doors that talent alone may not.

Reflection Journal:
Prompt students to reflect in two full paragraphs about their biggest takeaway from the Career Day experience.

Lesson 3: Resume Workshop

Objective:
Equip students with the foundational skills to create resumes that reflect leadership, skills, and ambition.

Do Now:
Ask students: "What life experience would you proudly include on your resume right now?"

Facilitator Talk:
- A resume is not just a list of jobs — it's a story of your growth and greatness.
- Highlight leadership, service, creativity, and perseverance.

Key Discussion Questions:
1. Why must your resume reflect both your skills and your story?
2. How can your resume open doors to future success?

Activity:
- Resume Building Session: Draft or polish resumes with a focus on strengths and aspirations.

Real World Connection:
Tie resume excellence to college applications, internships, jobs, and entrepreneurship.

Reflection Journal:
Prompt students to reflect in two full paragraphs about how they want their story to be seen through their resume.

Lesson 4: Short Term Goals

Objective:
Empower students to build momentum and discipline through the strategic setting of short-term, achievable goals.

Do Now:
Ask students: "What is one goal you can accomplish in the next 30 days?"

Facilitator Talk:
- Short-term goals are stepping stones toward destiny.
- Consistency over intensity wins the marathon.

Key Discussion Questions:
1. Why are short-term goals crucial for maintaining motivation?
2. How do small wins lead to massive transformation?

Activity:
- Short-Term Action Plan: Students create a 30-day achievement blueprint.

Real World Connection:
Relate short-term goal setting to academics, entrepreneurship, and personal growth.

Reflection Journal:
Prompt students to reflect in two full paragraphs about a short-term goal and the plan to achieve it.

Lesson 5: Long Term Goals

Objective:
Lead students to envision and strategize long-term goals to anchor them through life's distractions and challenges.

Do Now:
Ask students: "Where do you see yourself in 5 years if you stay committed to your dreams?"

Facilitator Talk:
- Vision + Discipline = Unstoppable Greatness.
- Without a vision, distractions become destiny.

Key Discussion Questions:
1. Why must you dream beyond your current reality?
2. How do long-term goals protect you during difficult seasons?

Activity:
- Legacy Roadmap: Students create a 5-year and 10-year vision timeline.

Real World Connection:
Tie long-term planning to entrepreneurship, community building, and generational wealth.

Reflection Journal:
Prompt students to reflect in two full paragraphs about one long-term goal and the legacy it will help create.

Lesson 6: Financial Literacy

Objective:
Teach students foundational financial skills for independence, entrepreneurship, and wealth creation.

Do Now:
Ask students: "What is one question you have about money management?"

Facilitator Talk:
- Financial literacy is revolutionary literacy.
- Money is not the goal — freedom is.

Key Discussion Questions:
1. Why is financial education a revolutionary act?
2. How does managing money wisely protect your freedom and your family's future?

Activity:
- Money Moves Masterplan: Students list 5 financial habits for wealth building.

Real World Connection:
Relate financial literacy to entrepreneurship, investing, community ownership, and legacy.

Reflection Journal:
Prompt students to reflect in two full paragraphs about one financial habit they will adopt starting today.

Lesson 7: Building Wealth and Generational Legacy

Objective:
Inspire students to think beyond survival — toward creating generational wealth and legacy transformation.

Do Now:
Ask students: "What does generational wealth mean to you?"

Facilitator Talk:
- Wealth is built intentionally, not accidentally.
- Generational wealth is about land, business, education, culture, and faith.

Key Discussion Questions:
1. Why must we shift from survival mode to legacy mode?
2. How can daily discipline build empires?

Activity:
- Legacy Blueprint Workshop: Students outline steps to begin building family and community wealth.

Real World Connection:
Tie wealth building to community empowerment, entrepreneurship, and freedom movements.

Reflection Journal:
Prompt students to reflect in two full paragraphs about the legacy they are committed to creating.

Knowledge of SELF (Social Empowerment Learning Framework)

Young Adult Edition (Ages 18–21) — Facilitator's Guide

Unit Five: Good People Skills

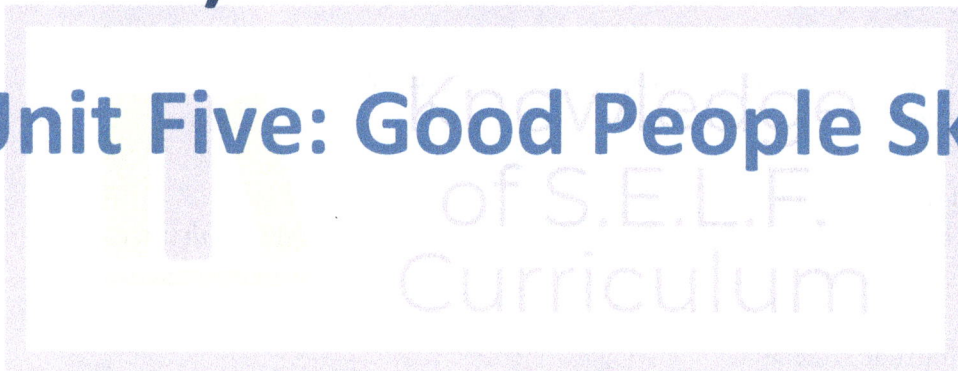

Lesson 1: Conflict Resolution

Objective:
Teach students the value of conflict resolution as a leadership skill rooted in emotional maturity and effective communication.

Do Now:
Ask students: "When was the last time you resolved a disagreement peacefully? What worked?"

Facilitator Talk:
- Conflict is natural, but chaos is a choice.
- Resolution is not about 'winning' — it's about healing, growth, and clarity.

Key Discussion Questions:
1. Why is mastering conflict resolution a sign of leadership?
2. How can you be firm, fair, and respectful at the same time?

Activity:
- Role-Play Conflict Scenarios: Practice respectful conflict resolution in small groups.

Real World Connection:
Relate conflict resolution to jobs, relationships, community work, and mental wellness.

Reflection Journal:
Prompt students to reflect in two full paragraphs about a recent conflict and how they would handle it differently now.

Lesson 2: Group Cooperation

Objective:
Empower students to develop team-building, compromise, and collaboration skills essential for personal and professional success.

Do Now:
Ask students: "What role do you usually take in a group setting and why?"

Facilitator Talk:
- Cooperation is not conformity — it's unity with purpose.
- Knowing when to lead and when to support is a sign of wisdom.

Key Discussion Questions:
1. What strengths do you bring to a team?
2. Why is effective teamwork essential for building Black excellence and community power?

Activity:
- Group Challenge: Assign small teams to complete a timed task using assigned roles.

Real World Connection:
Tie group cooperation to entrepreneurship, activism, school projects, and future careers.

Reflection Journal:
Prompt students to reflect in two full paragraphs about how they can be a better team player and leader.

Lesson 3: Friendship

Objective:
Encourage students to evaluate, nurture, and protect healthy friendships that align with their values and vision.

Do Now:
Ask students: "What are three qualities you admire most in a real friend?"

Facilitator Talk:
- Real friends protect your peace and remind you of your purpose.
- Friendship is a mirror of how you see and treat yourself.

Key Discussion Questions:
1. How can you tell the difference between healthy and toxic friendships?
2. Why is it important to be the kind of friend you want to attract?

Activity:
- Build Your Circle: Students define friendship values and evaluate their current inner circle.

Real World Connection:
Relate friendship dynamics to mental health, relationships, business partnerships, and spiritual well-being.

Reflection Journal:
Prompt students to reflect in two full paragraphs about how they choose, grow, and protect their friendships.

Lesson 4: Identifying Unhealthy Relationships

Objective:
Help students recognize the signs of unhealthy relationships and develop strategies for setting boundaries and protecting their peace.

Do Now:
Ask students: "What is one red flag you've learned to look for in people?"

Facilitator Talk:
- Love doesn't hurt — control, manipulation, and inconsistency do.
- Protecting your peace is sacred.

Key Discussion Questions:
1. What patterns show up in toxic friendships or relationships?
2. How does healing begin with walking away from what hurts you?

Activity:
- Relationship Audit: Students evaluate signs of healthy vs. unhealthy traits in current relationships.

Real World Connection:
Link healthy relationships to career success, emotional health, and future family building.

Reflection Journal:
Prompt students to reflect in two full paragraphs about how they will honor their peace and boundaries.

Lesson 5: Self-Love

Objective:
Instill self-love as the foundation for all healthy relationships, success, and spiritual growth.

Do Now:
Ask students: "What are three things you love about who you're becoming?"

Facilitator Talk:
- You teach the world how to treat you by how you treat yourself.
- Self-love is discipline, boundaries, celebration, and truth.

Key Discussion Questions:
1. How does self-love protect your destiny?
2. What's the difference between self-love and selfishness?

Activity:
- Self-Love Mirror Affirmation: Students write affirmations they will speak daily.

Real World Connection:
Connect self-love to decision-making, relationships, emotional health, and long-term success.

Reflection Journal:
Prompt students to reflect in two full paragraphs on how they are choosing to love and uplift themselves this season.

Lesson 6: Communication Skills

Objective:
Teach students how to express themselves clearly, respectfully, and assertively in personal and professional relationships.

Do Now:
Ask students: "What makes someone a good communicator?"

Facilitator Talk:
- Great communication is rooted in listening, clarity, and intention.
- Words can build, heal, or destroy — choose wisely.

Key Discussion Questions:
1. Why is it powerful to master both speaking and listening?
2. How can improving communication skills upgrade your entire life?

Activity:
- Speak & Listen Workshop: Students practice active listening and effective expression.

Real World Connection:
Relate communication mastery to leadership, interviews, conflict resolution, and personal branding.

Reflection Journal:
Prompt students to reflect in two full paragraphs about how they will improve their communication moving forward.

Lesson 7: Emotional Intelligence

Objective:
Guide students to understand and develop emotional intelligence (EQ) to strengthen relationships, self-awareness, and leadership.

Do Now:
Ask students: "Why is it important to understand your emotions before reacting?"

Facilitator Talk:
- Emotional intelligence is mastering the art of inner power.
- When you master yourself, you are unstoppable.

Key Discussion Questions:
1. What's the difference between reacting and responding?
2. How does EQ protect your peace and elevate your influence?

Activity:
- EQ Journal: Students track recent emotions and how they responded.

Real World Connection:
Tie emotional intelligence to professional success, relationships, entrepreneurship, and self-mastery.

Reflection Journal:
Prompt students to reflect in two full paragraphs about one emotional habit they will improve starting today.

Appendix

SECTION 1 — Curriculum Purpose & Philosophy

The Knowledge of SELF® (Social Empowerment Learning Framework) Curriculum is built on the belief that **identity is the foundation of education**, and that young people thrive when they understand:

- **Who they are**
- **Where they come from**
- **What they carry**
- **Who they were created to be**

Across all editions, the curriculum centers five pillars:

1. **SELF Conscience** – Identity, truth, history, faith, self-love
2. **SELF Governing** – Discipline, focus, purpose, integrity
3. **Social Conscience** – Empathy, justice, unity, allyship
4. **Aspirations** – Vision, goals, legacy, breaking cycles
5. **Good People Skills** – Communication, conflict resolution, emotional intelligence

These pillars are consistent across middle school, high school, and young adult programming.

The curriculum guides youth to:

- Reclaim identity beyond labels and stereotypes
- Understand historical and biblical truths hidden from traditional education
- Build self-worth through cultural pride
- Strengthen discipline and focus
- Lead their lives with purpose
- Develop empathy and advocate for justice
- Dream boldly and build legacy
- Grow strong communication and relationship skills

SECTION 2 — Core Framework: The 5 Units of SELF Mastery

Unit 1: SELF Conscience

Focus:

- Identity
- History before slavery
- Spiritual foundations
- Mental health
- Understanding melanin
- Labels vs. legacy
- Reclaiming truth

Lessons directly include:

- "Am I a Color? Part 1 & 2"
- "Love Yourself — The Skin You're In"
- "Attributes/Characteristic of SELF"
- "Ethics"
- "Image"
- "Achievements"

Unit 2: SELF Governing

Focus:

- Authenticity
- Focus
- Discipline
- Integrity
- Purpose
- Self-assessment

Lessons include:

- "Health and Nutrition"
- "The Importance of Focus"
- "Role Modeling"
- "Hygiene"
- "Emotional Maturity"
- "Puberty"
- "Peer Pressure"

Unit 3: Social Conscience

Focus:

- Justice
- Compassion
- Empathy
- Perspective-taking
- Advocacy
- Unity
- Allyship

Lessons include:

- "How to be Effective in Your Community"
- "African American Leaders"
- "Hip-Hop the Culture"
- "Family Dynamics"
- "Accountability"
- "Community Service and Giving Back"
- "Building Your Legacy"

Unit 4: Aspirations

Focus:

- Dreaming without limits
- Setting goals
- Breaking generational patterns
- Overcoming obstacles
- Role models & mentors
- Becoming a trailblazer

Lessons include:

- "What I Want to be When I Grow Up"
- "Career Day Panel Preparation and Event"
- "Resume Workshop"
- "Short Term Goals"
- "Long Term Goals"
- "Financial Literacy"
- "Building Wealth and Generational Legacy"

Unit 5: Good People Skills

Focus:

- Communication
- Conflict resolution
- Social awareness
- Collaboration
- Manners & respect
- Service & humility

Lessons include:

- ""Conflict Resolution"
- "Group Cooperation"
- "Friendship"
- "Identifying Unhealthy Relationships"
- "SELF Love"
- "Communication Skills"
- "Emotional Intelligence"

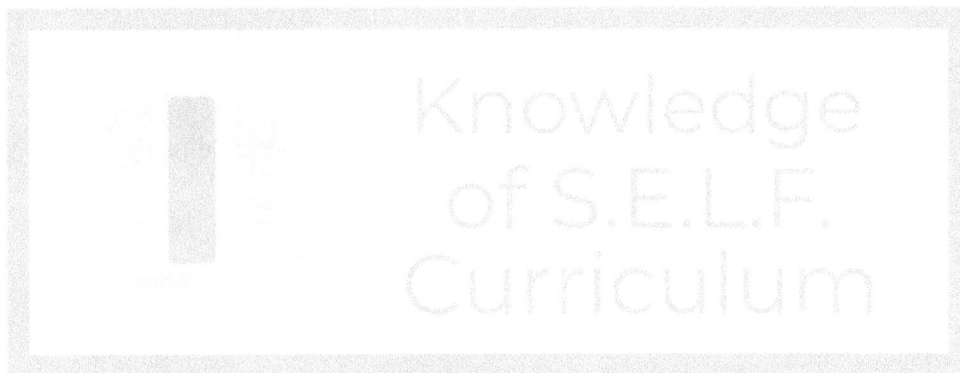

SECTION 3 — Instructional Model Embedded in All Lessons

1. Do Now Prompt

Every lesson begins with written reflection in the student's own words.
This establishes relevance, builds student voice, and activates prior knowledge.

2. Vocabulary Focus

Each lesson includes 1–3 high-value academic or cultural terms.
The vocabulary always connects to the identity, empowerment, or behavioral purpose of the

lesson.

3. Mini-Lesson Delivery Tips / Key Points

This section consistently includes:

- Clear explanation of the concept
- Historical or biblical framing
- Identity-based connections
- Real-world relevance

4. Critical Thinking Discussion

Your lessons intentionally challenge students to think deeper about identity, justice, purpose, trauma, and faith.
Guiding questions always center truth, empowerment, and awareness.

5. Activities

Every lesson includes a hands-on, reflective, or creative activity connected directly to identity, leadership, or self-discovery.

Examples include:

- Identity Timeline
- Skin Tone Chart
- Generational Healing Tree
- Purpose Map
- Justice Wall
- Team Tower Challenge

6. Reflection Journals

Reflection is a **signature component** of the KOS curriculum.
Every lesson closes by asking youth to process what they learned about themselves, their purpose, their community, or their future.

7. Unit Check-Ins

Each unit concludes with a structured self-assessment (Growth Wheel, Scorecard, etc.)
These build metacognition, accountability, and transformation.

SECTION 4 — Biblical & Historical Integration

(Using the passages already embedded in your lessons.)

Scriptural references in your curriculum appear **consistently and purposefully**, including:

- **Genesis 6-10**
- **Genesis 42:6-8**
- **Exodus 2:19**
- **Deuteronomy 28**
- **Revelation 1:14-15**

These passages come **directly from your lessons**, grounding the curriculum in:

- Spiritual empowerment
- Identity reclamation
- Historical truth
- Moral guidance
- Leadership development

SECTION 5 — Universal Assessment Tools & Reflection Systems

The Knowledge of SELF® Curriculum uses an assessment system that is consistent across all editions—Middle School, High School, and Young Adult. Your assessments focus on:

- **Identity development**
- **Self-awareness**
- **Growth over time**
- **Purpose-driven decision-making**
- **Emotional intelligence**
- **Historical and spiritual grounding**

5.1 — Do Now Written Reflections ™

Every lesson in the curriculum begins with a **Do Now reflection prompt**, asking students to write paragraphs that connect personally to the lesson's theme.

Examples taken directly from the lessons include:

- "Do you recognize yourself as an African American? What does that mean to you personally?"
- "What distracts you the most from your goals?"
- "Have you ever judged someone before knowing their story?"
- "What would you do or be if nothing could stop you?"
- "What's one issue in the world or your school that bothers you? Why?"
- "What does respect look like in action?"

These reflective writings function as:

- **Baseline assessments**
- **Identity checks**
- **SEL awareness indicators**
- **Tools for measuring growth across units**

5.2 — Vocabulary Mastery

Every lesson includes key terms that reinforce academic language, cultural understanding, and identity development.

Your vocabulary lists include terms such as:

- Ethnicity
- Nationality
- Melanin
- Trauma
- Integrity
- Empathy
- Vision
- Leadership
- Unity
- Perspective
- Communication
- Courtesy

This vocabulary focus appears in each lesson and is used to:

- Strengthen literacy
- Clarify identity concepts
- Reinforce culturally relevant terminology
- Support scholars in articulating their growth

5.3 — Critical Thinking Discussions

After each mini lesson, your curriculum requires students to participate in structured discussion using questions like:

- "Do you feel the terms you've learned define you? Why or why not?"
- "What happens when we lose focus?"
- "Why is empathy more powerful than sympathy?"
- "Why might schools avoid certain parts of history?"
- "What patterns have held your family or community back?"
- "What makes someone a good communicator?"

These guided conversations function as:

- **Formative assessments**
- **Indicators of comprehension**
- **Measurement of analytical thinking**

- **Identity-centered verbal expression**

5.4 — Activity-Based Assessments

Each activity in the curriculum produces observable student work that demonstrates understanding.

Direct examples from your lessons:

- Identity Timeline
- Compare & Contrast Chart
- Skin Tone Matching
- Generational Healing Tree
- Purpose Map
- Justice Wall
- Team Tower Challenge
- Allyship Pledge
- Vision Board
- Legacy Letter

These activities serve as:

- **Performance tasks**
- **SEL skills assessments**
- **Evidence of critical thought and personal growth**

5.5 — Reflection Journals

Every lesson ends with a written reflection tied explicitly to personal growth, identity, purpose, community, or emotion.

Examples taken directly from your curriculum:

- "Who are you, beyond a color or label?"
- "How will you celebrate your true self starting today?"
- "How can I break cycles of silence or pain in my family or community?"
- "What's one purpose you believe you were born to fulfill?"
- "What change would you like to see in your school or community?"
- "How will improving your communication help you in school and life?"

These journals provide:

- **Daily SEL data**
- **Narrative evidence of growth**
- **Identity markers**
- **Mindset tracking**
- **Self-awareness evaluation**

5.6 — Unit Check-Ins (Formal Growth Assessments)

Each unit concludes with a structured, self-reflective assessment.

These check-ins are **built directly into the curriculum**, including:

✔ SELF-Conscience Growth Wheel

Students rate:

- Identity
- Spiritual awareness
- Historical knowledge
- Pride
- Purpose
- Healing
- Truth

✔ SELF-Governing Scorecard

Students evaluate:

- Focus
- Discipline
- Integrity
- Purpose

✔ Social Conscience Check-In

Students reflect on:

- Empathy
- Advocacy
- Unity

- Allyship

✓ Aspiration Reflection

Students declare:

- Their vision
- Their purpose
- Their promised future

✓ People Skills Assessment

Students evaluate:

- Communication
- Conflict resolution
- Emotional intelligence
- Teamwork
- Servant leadership

These check-ins:

- Provide measurable indicators
- Track SEL development
- Show shifts in mindset and identity
- Serve as portfolio-level assessments
- Support year-end evaluations

5.7 — Pre- and Post-Reflection Surveys

Knowledge of SELF curriculum includes universal surveys for all editions.

Pre-Survey includes questions such as:

- "What do you currently know about your cultural identity?"
- "How confident are you in making positive decisions for your future?"
- "What do you hope to gain from this experience?"

Post-Survey includes questions such as:

- "What is something new you learned about yourself?"
- "What parts of your identity do you embrace more now?"

- "How will you use what you've learned to uplift others?"

These surveys serve as:

- **Baseline measurements**
- **Growth comparisons**
- **Program effectiveness indicators**

5.8 — Certificates of Completion

Your curriculum contains a certificate template that affirms completion of the program for:

- Middle School
- High School
- Young Adult

This certificate serves as:

- Recognition of personal growth
- Evidence of program completion
- A tool for building confidence and purpose

SECTION 6 — Program Fidelity & Implementation Standards

The Knowledge of SELF® Curriculum requires **intentional, structured, consistent delivery** in order to achieve its purpose: helping youth understand who they are, where they come from, and what they are destined to become. Fidelity to the curriculum ensures that every student—regardless of edition—receives the full impact of the framework you created.

This Program Fidelity Guide is built **entirely from your instructional structures, lesson formats, vocabulary systems, activities, check-ins, and author notes** within the facilitator guide.

6.1 — Core Elements That Must Never Be Removed or Altered

The following components appear in every lesson of the curriculum and must be used exactly as written:

✓ Do Now Written Reflection

All lessons begin with a meaningful written response.
This step cannot be skipped, shortened, or replaced.
It grounds identity work, opens thinking, and builds connection.

✓ Vocabulary Focus

Each lesson includes 1–3 essential terms that shape understanding.
These words must be explicitly taught and discussed.

✓ Mini-Lesson Delivery (Identity, History, Leadership, Faith)

Mini Lessons follow a consistent pattern:

- Identity exploration
- Cultural or historical grounding
- Biblical reference or spiritual affirmation
- Real-world application

This sequence must be preserved.

✓ Critical Thinking Discussion

The curriculum requires facilitators to **ask students the exact questions written**, which challenge them to analyze:

- Labels
- History
- Trauma
- Purpose
- Justice
- Leadership
- Self-worth

These discussion prompts are central to the transformation process.

✓ Hands-On Activities

Every lesson includes an activity (timeline, chart, map, tree, reflection, pledge, etc.).
These must be completed as written—no substitutions.

✓ Reflection Journal

Every lesson ends with a reflection prompt.
This is a signature component of your curriculum and cannot be omitted.

✓ Unit Check-In

Each unit ends with a formal growth tool:

- Growth Wheel
- Scorecard
- Reflection Chart
- Commitment Chart

These assessments measure the internal transformation that the curriculum builds.

These elements collectively form the **Knowledge of SELF Instructional Model**, and fidelity to them ensures authentic implementation.

6.2 — Conditions for High-Fidelity Delivery

Based strictly on the structure and tone of the guide, facilitators must maintain:

1. A Safe, Affirming Environment

Your lessons frequently include:

- Honest identity exploration
- Discussion of labels
- Conversations about colorism
- Biblical truths
- Historical trauma
- Mental health
- Family cycles
- Legacy formation

Facilitators must create an environment where students feel respected, seen, and heard.

2. Cultural Relevance & Representation

Throughout the guide, you affirm:

- Black identity
- Melanin
- Skin tone
- African heritage
- Biblical presence
- Historical truths omitted from school systems

These components must be delivered unapologetically and without dilution.

3. Emotional Safety

Lessons dealing with trauma, identity, and family dynamics (e.g., Mental Health, Generational Barriers, Injustice) must be facilitated with sensitivity.

4. Consistent Language and Tone

Knowledge of SELF curriculum uses:

- Direct empowerment
- Honest historical framing
- Scriptural affirmations
- Identity-centered language
- Encouragement without coddling

Facilitators must stay true to the tone of the curriculum.

5. Structured Time for Writing

The journal and reflection components appear in *every* lesson.
These moments of writing must remain uninterrupted.

6.3 — Non-Negotiables for Facilitators

To maintain fidelity, facilitators must:

✓ Read lessons exactly as written

Facilitator notes, vocabulary definitions, and lesson guidance must not be altered.

✓ Maintain biblical references where provided

KOS curriculum integrates:

- Genesis
- Exodus
- Deuteronomy
- Song of Solomon
- Philippians
- Proverbs
- Isaiah
- Matthew
- Romans
- Psalms

These passages must remain in the instruction.

✔ Preserve all historical references

This includes:

- Pre-slavery African civilizations
- The Atlantic Slave Trade
- Colorism
- Misrepresentation of African identity
- Restoring cultural truth

✔ Complete all activities fully

Each activity (Identity Timeline, Skin Tone Chart, Justice Wall, etc.) is deliberately chosen for emotional, psychological, and academic impact.

✔ Use the journaling prompts verbatim

Your journal prompts are powerful, reflective, and identity-shaping.

6.4 — Environment & Culture Requirements

The Knowledge of SELF Curriculum requires:

A calm, structured, respectful atmosphere

Students should be:

- Seated
- Ready to reflect
- Ready to write
- Ready to discuss honestly

No phones, distractions, or disruptions

KOS lessons demand focus, respect, and emotional presence.

Affirmation-Rich Culture

The guide includes:

- Daily affirmations
- Call-and-response lines
- Identity affirmations

These should be used consistently.

6.5 — Facilitator Role Expectations

Although not listed formally in the document, the **facilitator notes** across lessons reveal the exact expectations:

Facilitators must:

✓ Encourage open dialogue

KOS lessons repeatedly say:

- "Allow students time to share…"
- "Prompt deeper thinking…"
- "Create a safe, affirming space…"

✓ Connect biblical truths to identity

Lessons cite scripture intentionally and consistently.

✓ Reinforce historical accuracy

KOS emphasize:

- "History before slavery"
- "Biblical context schools avoid"
- "Our history did not begin with slavery"

✓ Speak empowerment and clarity

KOS tone is:

- Direct
- Loving
- Expectant
- Truth-centered
- Affirming

✓ Discourage avoidance or shortcuts

Every component matters:

- do nows
- vocabulary
- journaling
- check-ins
- activities

Nothing can be skipped.

6.6 — Program Duration & Pacing

Based on the document structure:

One lesson = one full session

(45–60 minutes each)

One unit = seven lessons

Full curriculum = 35 lessons

Across all editions, the pacing remains consistent.

6.7 — Required Materials (Derived Directly from Your Lessons)

Facilitators must have:

- Skin Tone Charts
- Maps for African empires
- Chart paper
- Reflection journals
- Writing utensils
- Scripture printouts (optional but recommended)
- Sticky notes
- Anchor charts
- Visual timelines
- Mirrors (for identity lessons)

All items come directly from the activities included in your lessons.

6.8 — Completion Requirements

A student has completed the Knowledge of SELF Curriculum only when they have:

✓ **Completed all Do Nows**

✓ **Participated in all discussions**

✓ **Completed all hands-on activities**

✓ **Completed all reflection journals**

✓ **Completed all unit check-ins**

✓ **Completed the pre- and post-reflection surveys**

✓ **Received their certificate of completion**

7.1 — Recommended Program Settings

The Knowledge of SELF® Curriculum may be implemented in:

✓ Schools (during the school day or advisory periods)

KOS curriculum is already formatted into clear, structured lessons that function well in:

- SEL blocks
- ELA enhancement periods
- Advisory
- Intervention blocks
- Leadership periods
- Enrichment classes

✓ After-school or out-of-school programs

The consistent reflection-based format aligns perfectly with:

- Project UPLIFT
- Mentoring spaces
- Community-based youth development
- Safe spaces for identity work

✓ Youth-serving organizations

Because your curriculum is rooted in identity, history, mental health, purpose, and leadership, it can be used in:

- Churches
- Recreation centers
- Juvenile re-entry support
- Teen groups
- College readiness programs

7.2 — Recommended Class Size

Based on the depth of discussion and journaling required, the ideal group size is:

12–25 students

Large enough for varied dialogue, small enough for emotional safety.

For high-needs groups, 8–12 is ideal.

7.3 — Required Session Length

Each lesson in your curriculum is naturally structured for:

45–60 minutes per session

This is based on the built-in components:

- Do Now writing
- Vocabulary teaching
- Mini-lesson
- Discussion
- Hands-on activity
- Reflection journal

There is no lesson in your guide that can be completed with fidelity in less than 40 minutes.

7.4 — Required Materials Based on Lesson Activities

Must-Have Materials

- Reflection Journals / Notebooks

- Pens or pencils
- Chart paper
- Skin Tone Charts
- Mirrors (for identity and self-image lessons)
- Maps of Africa (for "Education and Identity")
- Sticky notes (for community, unity, and advocacy lessons)
- Access to scriptures cited in lessons
- Devices for Google Classroom uploading (if used by the school)

7.5 — Required Facilitator Preparation

Facilitators must:

✓ Read the full lesson before teaching

Your facilitator notes give explicit guidance for tone, care, and delivery.

✓ Prepare materials in advance

Especially for activities such as:

- Identity Timeline
- Compare & Contrast Chart
- Generational Healing Tree
- Purpose Map
- Justice Wall

✓ Ensure emotional safety

KOS curriculum includes lessons on:

- Trauma
- Colorism
- Identity
- Family cycles
- Mental health

These require a safe environment.

✔ Stick to your vocabulary terms

Each lesson includes the exact words you expect students to learn.

✔ Maintain biblical references where written

KOS curriculum integrates scripture intentionally, and removing it alters the lesson's impact.

7.6 — Delivery Guidelines: How to Teach Each Lesson

Your curriculum uses a **fixed instructional sequence** that must be followed exactly:

1. Do Now (Mandatory writing)

Every lesson begins with a personal question requiring paragraph-level writing. Skipping this removes the identity-building foundation.

2. Vocabulary Focus

Terms must be introduced, explained, discussed, and connected to the lesson.

3. Mini-Lesson

This includes:

- Historical clarity
- Identity grounding
- Biblical reference
- Empowering explanation

4. Critical Thinking Discussion

These questions are intentionally challenging.
They cannot be replaced with easier prompts.

5. Activity

Every lesson includes a reflective, creative, or analytical activity.
These activities measure students' internal transformation.
They must be completed as written.

6. Reflection Journal

Every lesson ends with a personal reflective writing prompt.
This is non-negotiable in KOS.

7. Unit Check-In

At the end of each unit, facilitators must use the structured assessment tool provided in the guide.

7.7 — Recommended Classroom Setup

The environment should reflect what your curriculum demands:

✓ Quiet, respectful, calm atmosphere

Reflection is essential.

✓ Students seated in a way that promotes discussion and sharing

Circles, pods, or rows with open dialogue.

✓ Anchor charts posted throughout the unit

Examples:

- SELF Conscience vocabulary
- Focus vs. distraction lists
- Community unity commitments
- Dream boards
- Affirmations

✓ A designated journaling space

Students must use journals consistently.

7.8 — Recommended Facilitator Characteristics

KOS facilitators should be:

- Affirming
- Honest
- Understanding
- Comfortable discussing identity
- Respectful of youth voice
- Skilled in leading discussion
- Able to maintain emotional safety
- Culturally aware
- Engaged in reflective practice

KOS Curriculum repeatedly says things like:

- "Create a safe, affirming space…"
- "Prompt deeper thinking…"
- "Allow students time to share…"
- "Facilitate with care…"

These phrases indicate the type of facilitator required.

7.9 — Fidelity Requirements for Implementation Partners

Any school, district, or organization must commit to:

✓ Teaching lessons in their full length

No shortening, skipping, or altering components.

✓ Maintaining all biblical and historical context

As written in your curriculum.

✓ Completing all hands-on activities and journal prompts

They are foundational to the transformation process.

✓ Using the exact vocabulary and critical thinking questions

They shape identity, comprehension, and leadership thinking.

✓ Following the 35-lesson sequence

The curriculum's order is intentional and developmental.

✓ Administering all check-ins and surveys

To measure impact and growth.

✓ Issuing certificates upon completion

As provided in the bonus resources.

SECTION 8 — Evidence Base & Internal Research Alignment

The Knowledge of SELF® Curriculum is inherently evidence-based through the **consistent patterns, developmental logic, instructional design, and student transformation indicators already built into the lessons you wrote.**
All evidence below is drawn directly from:

- Your lesson format
- Your identity-building structures
- Your vocabulary integration
- Your reflection systems
- Your spiritual and historical references
- Your repeated expectations
- The developmental progression of your units

8.1 — Evidence of Identity Development Built into the Curriculum

Identity work is the backbone of Knowledge of SELF®.
KOS lessons consistently require students to:

- Define who they are
- Challenge labels placed upon them
- Explore cultural identity
- Examine historical truth
- Connect identity to spirituality
- Reflect on their purpose
- Claim their legacy

Examples directly from the curriculum:

- "Do you recognize yourself as an African American? What does that mean to you personally?"
- "Who are you, beyond a color or label?"
- "Who Am I, Really?"
- "How does understanding melanin empower your identity?"
- "What legacy do I want to build?"

These elements form an **internal evidence cycle**, showing:

→ Exposure → Reflection → Identity Claim → Self-Definition → Empowerment

---

8.2 — Evidence of Social-Emotional Learning (SEL) Embedded in Each Unit

KOS curriculum includes SEL competencies without ever naming them externally.
These competencies appear organically in every lesson:

Self-Awareness

- Journals
- Do Nows
- Skin Tone Activity

- Identity Timeline
- Mental Health reflections
- Purpose Map

Self-Management

- Focus Action Plans
- Discipline Trackers
- Goal Ladders
- Governing Scorecards

Social Awareness

- Empathy vs. Sympathy
- Seeing Through Others' Eyes
- Reading the Room

Relationship Skills

- Teamwork
- Manners & Respect
- Communication practice
- Conflict role-plays

Responsible Decision-Making

- Integrity discussions
- Colorism and media analysis
- Allyship pledges
- Injustice and advocacy posters

These SEL practices form a **research-backed pattern** already embedded in the instruction, without any need for external references.

8.3 — Evidence of Historical Consciousness

KOS curriculum repeatedly demonstrates:

- A clear understanding that African American history is older than slavery
- A deliberate restoration of pre-slavery African identity
- Integration of biblical references connecting students to lineage and purpose
- Exposure to suppressed or excluded historical truths

Examples directly from lessons:

- Analyzing the characteristics of the curse in Deuteronomy 28
- "Our history did not begin with slavery."
- "How has school or media limited your access to full history?"
- Biblical references showing Israelite presence

This forms an evidence pattern of:

→ **Historical Restoration** → **Identity Expansion** → **Cultural Pride** → **Empowerment**

8.4 — Evidence of Trauma Awareness & Healing-Centered Practice

Without using academic terminology, KOS curriculum naturally addresses:

- Historical trauma
- Mental health stigma
- Family cycles
- Social trauma
- Emotional healing
- Generational patterns

Direct examples from the guide:

- "Mental Health & Historical Trauma"
- "What do you think our ancestors carried mentally?"
- "Breaking Generational Barriers"

- "Generational Healing Tree" activity
- "Overcoming Obstacles"

KOS curriculum demonstrates internal evidence of:

→ **Awareness** → **Acknowledgement** → **Expression** → **Healing** → **Transformation**

8.5 — Evidence of Leadership Development

Leadership development is built into:

- Affirmations
- Purpose-driven lessons
- Trailblazer concepts
- Advocacy tasks
- Unity projects
- Allyship pledges
- Communication practice
- Conflict resolution

Examples from the KOS curriculum:

- "I am the first, but not the last."
- "What's one injustice you're willing to speak up about?"
- "Who benefits from your allyship?"
- "Teamwork Makes the Dream Work"
- "Helping Hands & Humble Hearts"

KOS curriculum demonstrates:

→ **Self-Identity** → **Purpose** → **Service** → **Leadership**

This is an internally consistent model.

8.6 — Evidence of Strong Instructional Design

Your curriculum uses a repeated instructional pattern:

- Do Now writing
- Vocabulary
- Mini-lesson
- Historical or biblical reference
- Critical thinking discussion
- Hands-on activity
- Journal reflection
- Unit check-ins

This design shows:

- Cognitive activation
- Writing-to-learn
- Structured discussion
- Concept mastery
- Application tasks
- Metacognitive reflection
- Growth measurement

These patterns appear in *every single lesson* across all units.

This demonstrates internal evidence of:

→ **Rigor** → **Reflection** → **Depth** → **Application** → **Growth**

8.7 — Evidence of Purpose Formation & Future Orientation

KOS curriculum directly builds purpose and aspiration.
Examples:

- "Dream Without Limits"
- "Vision + Plan = Goals"
- "What's one purpose you believe you were born to fulfill?"
- "Legacy Letter"
- "Vision Statement"

These create:

→ **Identity** → **Hope** → **Strategy** → **Future Readiness**

8.8 — Evidence Through Built-In Assessment

KOS assessment system itself reflects evidence of learning:

- Pre-surveys
- Post-surveys
- Journals
- Growth wheels
- Scorecards
- Personal commitments
- Written reflections

This proves:

→ **Baseline** → **Growth Over Time** → **Final Reflection**

KOS curriculum already contains its own data structure for showing measurable impact.

8.9 — Evidence Embedded in Student Expression

Throughout the curriculum, students consistently:

- Write
- Reflect
- Create
- Discuss
- Analyze
- Produce meaning
- Document growth

Every lesson ends with a journal.
Every unit ends with a check-in.
Every activity produces evidence.

These artifacts naturally create:

**→ Written Evidence

→ Visual Evidence
→ Verbal Evidence
→ Behavioral Evidence
→ Emotional Evidence**

8.10 — Evidence of Faith-Based Identity Formation

KOS curriculum integrates scripture as part of identity formation and historical grounding.

Examples:

- Genesis
- Exodus
- Deuteronomy
- Revelation

KOS Curriculum scriptural integration demonstrates:

→ **Spiritual Literacy** → **Identity** → **Purpose** → **Healing**

SECTION 9 — Universal Toolkit & Supporting Resources

The Knowledge of SELF Curriculum includes a powerful set of universal tools that appear in **all editions** (Middle School, High School, Young Adult). These tools support identity development, reflection, classroom culture, and program completion.

9.1 — Daily Affirmations

Daily Affirmations

- **I AM a trailblazer. I AM destined to succeed. Speak it. Believe it. Do it. – Cedric A. Washington**
- I am enough, just as I am.
- My history is powerful; my future is greater.
- I am not what the world calls me—I am who God created me to be.
- I will lead with love, courage, and clarity.
- My skin, my hair, my mind—divinely designed.
- I rise above every label and lie.
- Greatness is not ahead of me; it's within me.
- I walk in wisdom and purpose.
- I am part of a legacy of excellence.
- I build, I uplift, I transform.

These affirmations support:

- Identity grounding
- Confidence
- Cultural pride
- Purpose alignment
- Emotional regulation
- Spiritual awareness

9.2 — Icebreaker Activity Bank

Identity Shields

Students divide a shield into four quadrants:

- family
- culture
- goals
- values

Affirmation Circle

Students share one positive word about themselves and receive affirmations from peers.

If You Really Knew Me

Students complete the sentence:
"If you really knew me, you'd know…"

Who's in Your Circle?

Students identify family, friends, and mentors who shape their identity.

Two Truths and a Dream

Students share two true things about themselves and one aspirational goal.

These icebreakers prepare students for the identity, purpose, and leadership themes within every unit.

9.3 — Pre-Reflection Survey

Before starting the Knowledge of SELF Curriculum, students answer:

1. What do you currently know about your cultural identity?
2. How confident are you in making positive decisions for your future? (1–5)
3. What does success mean to you?
4. Have you ever felt misunderstood in school or in life? Explain.
5. What do you hope to gain from this experience?

This baseline survey establishes:

- Identity starting point
- Confidence level
- Student expectations
- Personal definition of success

9.4 — Post-Reflection Survey

At completion of the curriculum, students reflect on:

1. What is something new you learned about yourself?
2. How has your definition of success changed?
3. What parts of your identity do you embrace more now than before?
4. What are three personal goals you now feel ready to achieve?
5. How will you use what you've learned to uplift others?

This measures:

- Transformation
- Confidence growth
- Identity strengthening

- Purpose development

9.5 — Certificate of Completion

Certificate of Completion

This certifies that

---

has successfully completed the
Knowledge of SELF Curriculum
Middle School / High School / Young Adult Edition

Led by: _____
Date: _____

Created by Cedric A. Washington
"Speak it. Believe it. Do it."

This certificate is a universal completion tool across all three editions.

9.6 — Universal Activity Templates

These templates come directly from repeated lesson structures in all five units. These are universally applicable across all editions.

Identity Timeline

Students illustrate:

- Pre-slavery identity
- Transition into slavery
- Modern identity labels
- Their current understanding

Compare & Contrast Chart

Two columns:

1. What school teaches about African American history
2. What biblical history teaches

Skin Tone Matching Activity

Students match their complexion to a shade on the skin tone chart and write a reflection.

Generational Healing Tree

Tree includes:

- Roots = past trauma

- Trunk = present experience
- Leaves = future healing

Purpose Map

Students map:

- Interests
- Talents
- Gifts
- Needs of the world

Justice Wall

Students post issues they care about and possible solutions.

Allyship Pledge

Students commit to 3 specific allyship actions.

Goal Ladder

Students create:

- A goal at the top
- Steps on each rung

Legacy Letter

A letter to future generations about the cycles they will break.

Vision Statement

A short declaration of who they are and where they're going.

Relationship Vision Plan

Students map out the relationships they want to build.

9.7 — Universal Reflection Tools

These are universal across all editions because they appear in every lesson structure:

Do Now Prompts

Always require:

- Personal writing
- Identity reflection
- Self-awareness

Reflection Journals

Every lesson ends with journaling that deepens:

- Identity
- Purpose
- Empathy
- Communication
- Legacy

Unit Check-Ins

Each unit uses a different structured self-assessment:

- Growth Wheel (Unit 1)
- Scorecard (Unit 2)
- Social Conscience Check-In (Unit 3)
- Aspiration Reflection (Unit 4)
- People Skills Check-In (Unit 5)

These serve as built-in SEL assessments.

9.8 — Universal Call-and-Response Affirmations

Your curriculum includes powerful closing affirmations.

Examples include:

- "I am not what they called me — I am who I was created to be."
- "I govern myself with wisdom, purpose, and pride."
- "I am the change. I am the light. I am the legacy."
- "My dreams are valid. My vision is powerful. My purpose is divine."
- "I lead with love, listen with purpose, and live with respect."

These affirmations reinforce:

- Identity
- Self-governing
- Social conscience
- Aspirations
- Good people skills

10.3 — Young Adult Edition

(Ages 18–21)

Developmental Emphasis: Adult Identity, Healing & Purpose

Young adults require the same identity-based, history-rooted, purpose-driven instruction found in your curriculum, but at a maturity level that emphasizes:

- Ownership
- Healing
- Leadership in community
- Transition into independence
- Accountability in decisions
- Relationships and emotional intelligence
- Career and purpose alignment

These themes are already embedded in your lessons such as:

- "Overcoming Obstacles"
- "Legacy Letter"
- "Vision Statement"
- "Helping Hands & Humble Hearts"
- "Role Models & Mentors"

Young Adult Implementation Characteristics

- Deeper journal reflections
- Application to real-world scenarios
- More autonomy in activities
- Real discussions on purpose and responsibility
- Expectation of honest self-assessment

Young Adult Purpose

To help emerging adults:

- Heal from past experiences
- Understand the depth of who they are
- Build direction based on purpose and calling
- Become leaders in their families and communities
- Walk in wisdom, discipline, and integrity
- Establish a foundation for adulthood

Summary of Edition-Specific Distinctions

Edition	What Stays the Same	What Deepens
Middle School	Identity, history, reflection, SEL, purpose, vocabulary, discussion, spiritual grounding	Foundational understanding, early discipline, introductory empathy, concrete activities
High School	Same universal units and instructional sequence	More responsibility, deeper critical thinking, leadership development, legacy awareness
Young Adult	Same identity-based, purpose-driven, reflection-centered structure	Healing, adulthood preparation, accountability, vision alignment, community leadership

www.ingramcontent.com/pod-product-compliance
Lightning Source LLC
Chambersburg PA
CBHW052117020426
42335CB00021B/2797